D1289526

THE VICTORIA AND ALBERT COLOUR BOOKS

LIBRARY OF CONGRESS CATALOGING-IN-PUBLICATION DATA
MAIN ENTRY UNDER TITLE:

THE VICTORIA AND ALBERT COLOUR BOOK OF INDIAN FLORAL PATTERNS.

(THE V&A COLOUR BOOKS)
1. DECORATION AND ORNAMENT—PLANT FORMS—INDIA.
2. VICTORIA AND ALBERT MUSEUM. I. VICTORIA AND ALBERT
MUSEUM. II. TITLE: COLOUR BOOK OF INDIAN FLORAL PATTERNS.
III. SERIES.
NK1476.A1V5 1986  745.4'4954  85-19934
ISBN 0-8109-1714-9

COPYRIGHT © WEBB & BOWER (PUBLISHERS) LIMITED, EXETER,
THE TRUSTEES OF THE VICTORIA AND ALBERT MUSEUM, LONDON,
COOPER THIRKELL LIMITED, LONDON 1985

BOOK, COVER, AND SLIPCASE DESIGN BY COOPER THIRKELL LIMITED

PRODUCTION BY NICK FACER

PUBLISHED IN 1986 BY HARRY N. ABRAMS, INCORPORATED, NEW YORK
ALL RIGHTS RESERVED. NO PART OF THE CONTENTS OF THIS BOOK MAY BE
REPRODUCED WITHOUT THE WRITTEN PERMISSION OF THE PUBLISHERS
PRINTED AND BOUND IN HONG KONG

THE VICTORIA AND ALBERT COLOUR BOOKS

# INDIAN FLORAL
# PATTERNS

HARRY N. ABRAMS, INC., PUBLISHERS
NEW YORK

DURING the reign of the fifth Mughal emperor of India,* Shah Jahan (r. 1628-56), a remarkable decorative style was established. The emperor was an energetic patron of architecture, creating, for instance, a new city at Delhi called Shahjahanabad and rebuilding the citadel at Agra. The materials used were red sandstone and white marble, carved or inlaid with a style of ornamentation which had never been seen before. Flowering plants were carved in low relief into the soft sandstone, or inlaid in semi-precious stones such as lapis lazuli, carnelian and green jade to form a brilliant contrast with the marble. Amongst the flowers were tiny insects, butterflies, and Chinese clouds. Other buildings, particularly those in the north of the empire, were adorned with polychrome tilework, the design consisting of attenuated plant forms on a vivid yellow or green ground and contained within ornate cartouches.

Miniatures of the period show the theme was extended within the royal interiors: they depict wall hangings and carpets which echo the architectural motifs of plants in neatly arranged rows or within trellises, or used arch-like frames to enclose a single example. Courtly dress had naturalistic or purely imaginary flowers embroidered or woven into its design, the myriad colours of the flowers lavishly embellished with gold. Even the artefacts of the court harmonised with the new style, often using the same colour scheme as that found in the buildings. Gold boxes were covered with enamel and precious stones, white enamel forming the ground to flowers enamelled in translucent green and set with ruby and diamond 'petals'. The daggers which many at court wore tucked into their sashes had crystal or jade hilts carved with leafy scrolls or flower-heads, motifs often repeated in gold on the steel blades.

Floral decoration in itself was not, of course, unknown before this period; the innovation in Shah Jahan's reign was that it completely dominated the Mughal style. In the reign of Shah Jahan's grandfather, Akbar (r. 1556-1605), the conventions used for depicting flowers, trees and plants had been derived almost entirely from Iranian painting; in miniatures produced in Akbar's busy painting studios, the flowering plants show scattered across the landscape in isolated clumps all drew on a limited repertoire of leaf forms which were combined at random with a variety of realistic or, more usually, purely stylised flower heads. The same method was used on carved decoration on architecture. In Akbar's short-lived city of Fatehpur Sikri (built between 1571 and 1585) the dadoes of the 'Turkish Sultana's house', for example, are covered with trees and plants reproduced exactly from miniature painting.

At the same time realism in depicting the outside world was beginning to influence the way people and animals in particular were represented in painting, and this trend was to become more significant under Jahangir (r. 1605-27). The animals in the manuscript illustrations produced for

Akbar had often been identifiable and he also began to commission portraits of prominent figures at court. With Jahangir's reign, the emphasis in painting shifted from the production of manuscripts to studies of individual subjects set into albums, with particular painters becoming known for particular genres. The emperor's keen interest in the natural world, revealed in his autobiography the *Tuzuk-i Jahangiri,* was reflected in the carefully detailed paintings of exotic animals such as the zebra, or birds such as the turkey cock, both brought from abroad. The flora and fauna of India was also used as fit material for this kind of study. An important outside influence significantly

changed the representation of flowers during this period, however. European herbals were finding their way into the royal libraries, brought by the increasing numbers of traders, missionaries, emissaries and adventurers arriving at court and anxious to present the emperor with a gift which would attract his attention. The illustrations in the books were then copied by the court painters in the same way that they copied Western engravings of religious scenes, or the portrait of James I of England brought by his ambassador Sir Thomas Roe to the Mughal court in 1615. Under this new influence, Mughal flowers now move away from the conventions of Iranian painting to new, though in their own way, equally stylised formulae.

In the herbals, the flowers on a particular plant are typically shown both frontally and from the side, with the different stages of the blossoming of the flower given on the same plant. The flowers now seen in Mughal painting follow this pattern whether they are the subject of single studies painted by nature specialists such as Mansur, or are used in regularly spaced rows to form the borders to a central painting or calligraphic panel. These are then used in exactly the same way on architecture and in the decorative arts under Shah Jahan. The carved marble panels of the Taj Mahal, for instance, are essentially a series of flower studies of the format used in miniature painting linked horizontally within a decorative border. The frieze could also be translated into inlays on wood or metal artefacts, or onto textiles. The single plants seem completely naturalistic: flowers such as narcissus, poppies, irises, lilies and tulips can be recognised. It is clear, though, that the artists and craftsmen who used the motifs were not using real life to inspire their designs – virtually none of the flowers is botanically accurate in every respect, their forms are subtly repetitious and their representation is essentially decorative.

The question which remains is why the flower patterns which were used so much in Jahangir's paintings should now dominate the arts so completely. The answer seems to be to do with the very specific imperial image that Shah Jahan wished to project through his buildings, their adornment and by means of the artefacts which surrounded him. Recent research analysing the Persian architectural inscriptions shows that there are frequent allusions to Paradise which, in the conventions of Persian literature, is seen as a beautiful garden. Each building and its setting is intended to evoke an earthly Paradise. This idea in itself is not new – earlier Mughal buildings such as the tomb of the emperor Humayun (built at Delhi in 1564), had been set in gardens in the Iranian style with the same intention. However, the

architecture of Shah Jahan's reign and the decorative arts at all levels pick up and emphasise the theme to an extent which is overwhelming and which is certainly not accidental. The Persian verse on the Hall of Private Audience in the Fort at Delhi is to be taken almost literally: 'If there is Paradise on Earth, It is this, it is this, it is this.'

The floral style having been established, it was to remain dominant in the art of Mughal India. Connoisseurs such as Dara Shikuh, the son of Shah Jahan, also commissioned his painters to produce single studies of flowers – some, recognisably true to life; others, fantastic inventions with brightly coloured blooms of different types on the same stem. Between 1633 and 1642 he assembled these in a magnificent album which also included miniature paintings and calligraphy and which is now in the India Office Library. This album was the high point in the development of floral decoration but a comparable level of excellence, both of design and execution, is also found in other royal albums in which miniature paintings and calligraphy were surrounded by exquisite floral borders, often irrespective of their compatibility with the subject of the painting. One of the most beautiful floral borders in an album of the Shah Jahan period, known as the Minto Album and now in the Victoria and Albert Museum, surrounds a gruesome portrait of a Mughal noble brandishing the gory head of a rebel. The tradition of filling the margins of album pages with unrelated

decoration had been established in sixteenth century Iran, when calligraphic panels were surrounded by gold landscapes and animals, usually on a dark-coloured background. The Mughal illuminators took over this technique and adapted it to the new floral style to great effect.

During the reign of Shah Jahan's son Aurangzeb (r.1658-1707), the flower borders changed their appearance. The individual plants had become smaller and botanically less recognisable. They continued to be pre-eminent in album decoration, but were reduced to repeated motifs, albeit attractive ones, in contrast with the more individualistic floral elements in the Shah Jahan period borders. The use of gold paint for outlining the flowers and for drawing alternating sprigs of leaves remained popular. In the decorative arts too, floral motifs were becoming less well-defined.

The resilience of the flower theme in Indian art is seen in a book of flower patterns also in the V & A. Here, incongruously, the repeating floral element has become the main subject of the album: in a surprising change of rôle, the borders have taken over and are masquerading as miniature paintings. The painting of the patterns is in fact identical in technique to that of Mughal miniatures, being built up in several layers to produce opacity and depth of colour. The floral designs having usurped the main field of the album pages, the artist appears somewhat at a loss with regard to the borders: they are mostly composed of small gold sprigs, silver meandering vines, or sometimes quite unprecedented patterns with serpentine or fish-scale designs. The flowering plant motif, directly descended from the small-scale Aurangzeb-period border decoration, has at once been elevated to prominence in an album of its own, while at the same time being demoted by the 'sampler' format of some of the pages.

The book was put together as a royal Mughal album would have been, based on a system of carefully planned alternating double pages. In this case, the patterned pages are bordered with gold, and alternate with blank pages with silver borders. These pages were probably left empty because in some cases the pattern on the reverse would show through. In the painted pages, the dominant colour of the motifs on one side sometimes echoes the background of its partner, which might show a similar motif enlarged in size. Alternatively, the two halves of the double page might both show similar patterns but in different colours, or a single page might be divided by a wavy line into two contrasting colour schemes using the same basic motif. In some cases, the composition does stand as a work of art in its own right. The designs were intended primarily as textile patterns: some of the floral repeats are obviously appropriate to brocade and silk-weaving and some, particularly the striped designs, occur in the fine Kashmiri fabric used for the men's high-collared coats known as *jama.* The range of colours used, including bright purple, orange, and green, suggest use in textiles or painted decoration such as manuscript illustration rather than the more sober arts of architecture or metalwork. Many of the motifs could be painted on to wooden boxes or delicate glass huqqas or bottles. A small number of arabesque designs within medallions would have been used as stamped or painted ornament for bookbinding.

The book uses the form of the traditional Mughal album but its purpose is now essentially practical. It can be taken on its own merits as a book to be enjoyed, but as also clearly intended as a pattern book for craftsmen and clients. Thus the album has moved from the realm of kings into the world of merchants, while still retaining something of the spirit of its royal antecedents. Though the primary role of the flower patterns here is for use in other media, they still recall the days when they were painted for the Emperor's pleasure as decoration of royal album pages.

*'India' is used here to correspond to the Hindustan of the Mughal period. In Shah Jahan's reign, this included the northern part of modern India and parts of Afghanistan, and extended from Pakistan in the West to Bangladesh in the East.

FURTHER READING

*The Indian Heritage. Court Life and Arts under Mughal Rule,* catalogue of an exhibition held at the Victoria and Albert Museum from 21 April-15 August, 1982

Wayne E. Begley, 'The Symbolic Role of Calligraphy on Three Imperial Mosques of Shah Jahan' in *Kaladarsana. American Studies in the Art of India* ed. by J. G. Williams, New Delhi, 1981, pp. 7-18

Robert Skelton, 'A decorative motif in Mughal art' *Aspects of Indian Art* ed. by P. Pal, Leiden, 1972, pp. 147-52

THE PLATES

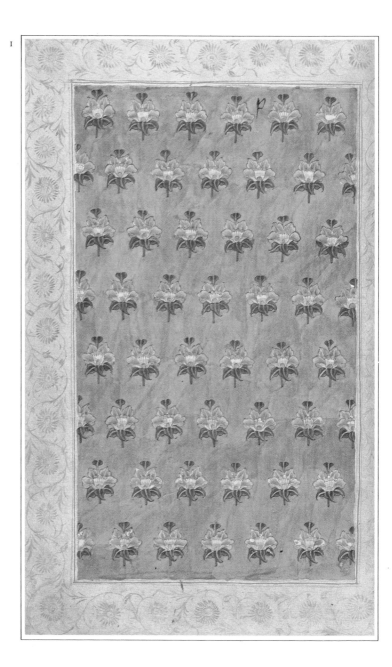

2

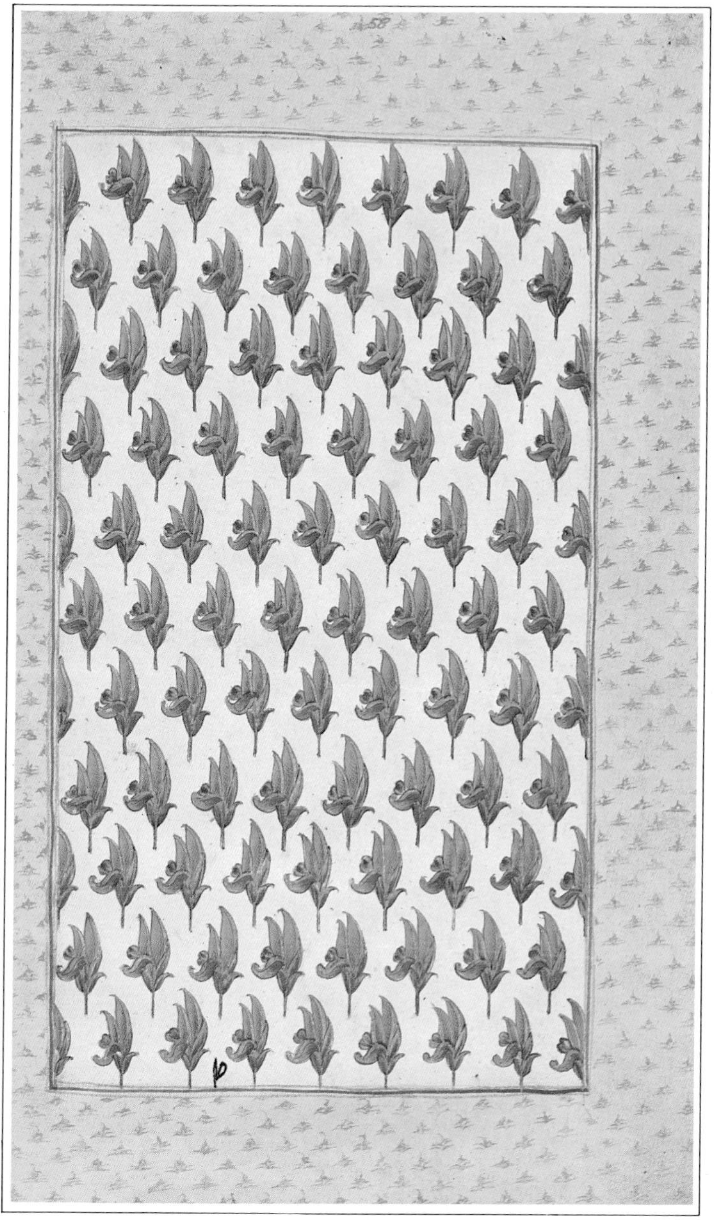

4

7

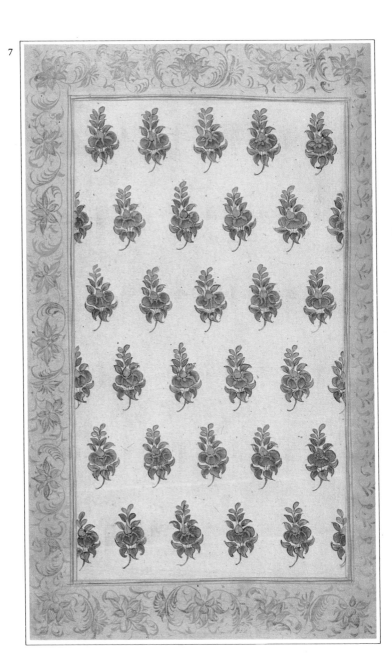

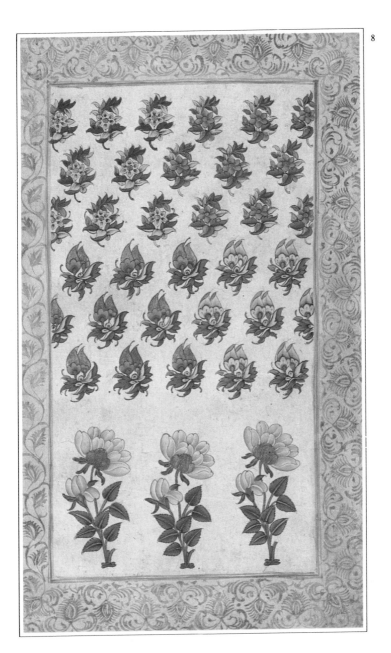

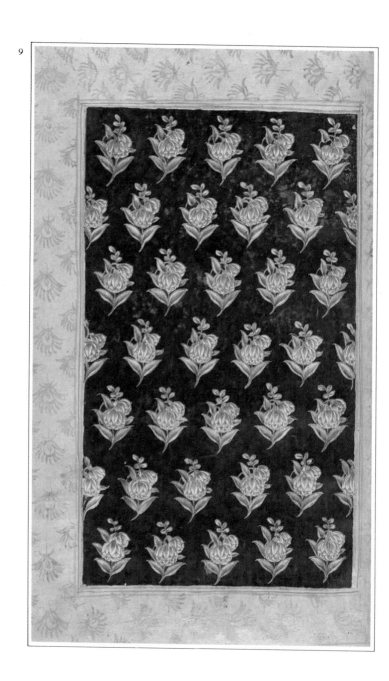

11

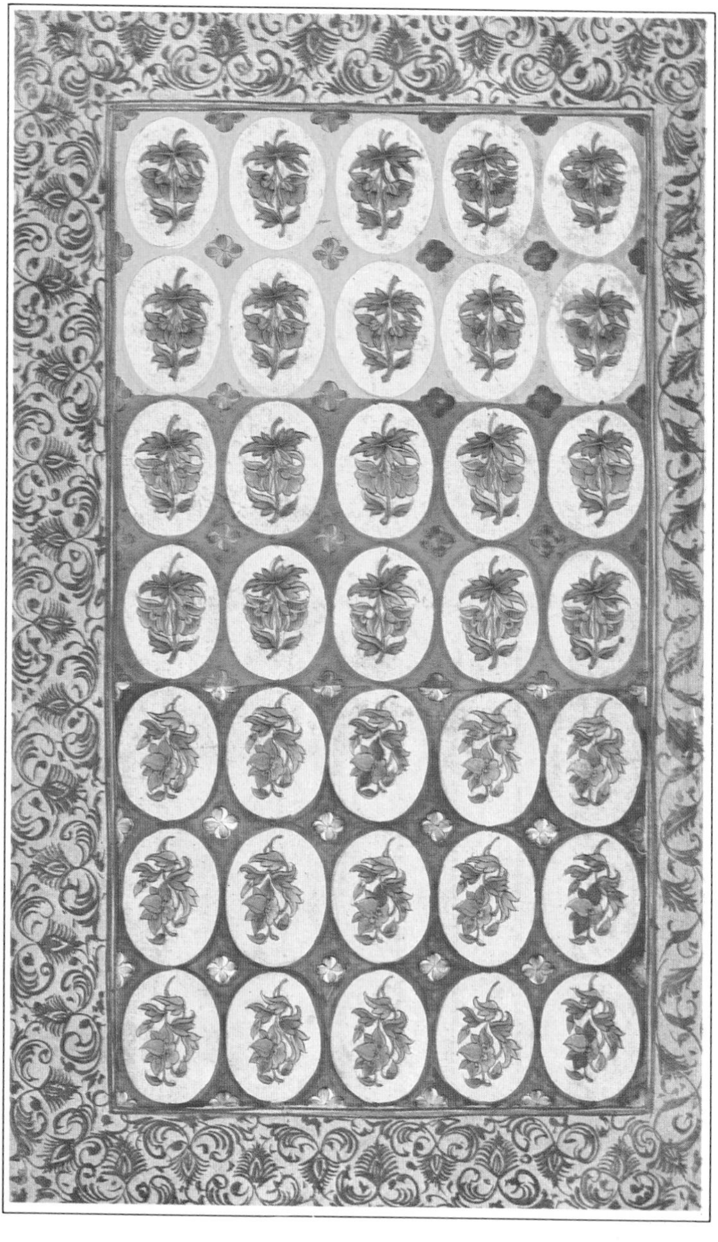

13

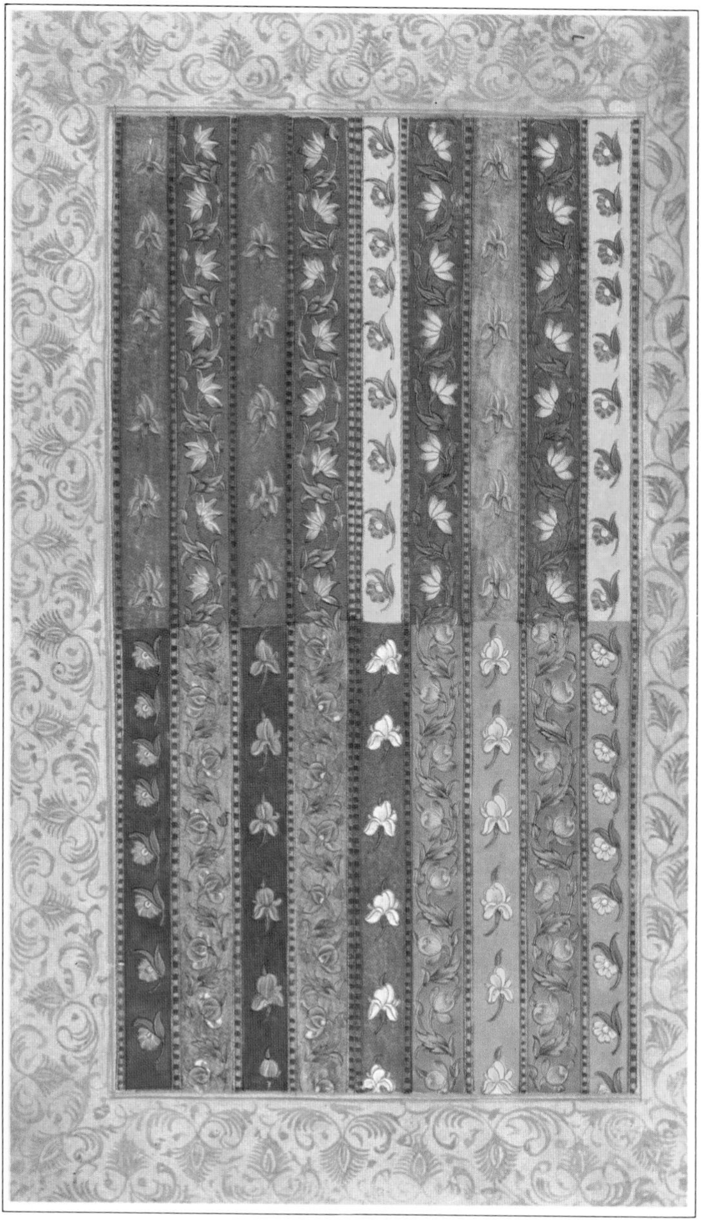

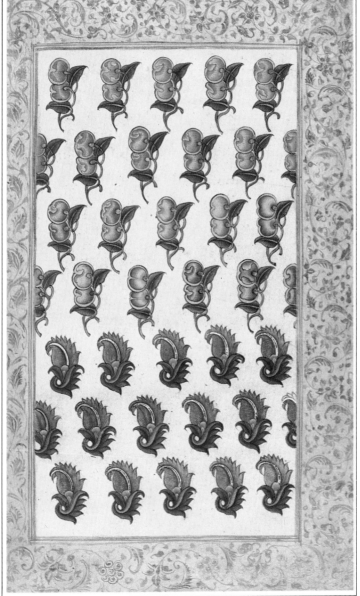

15

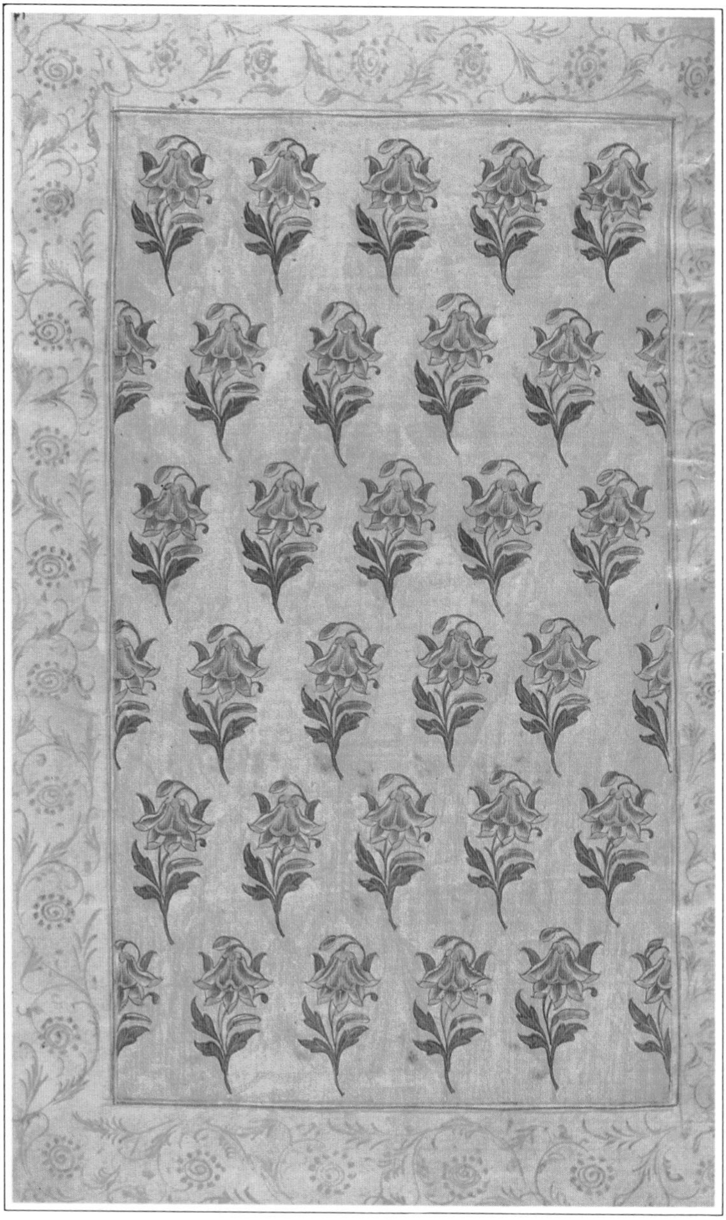

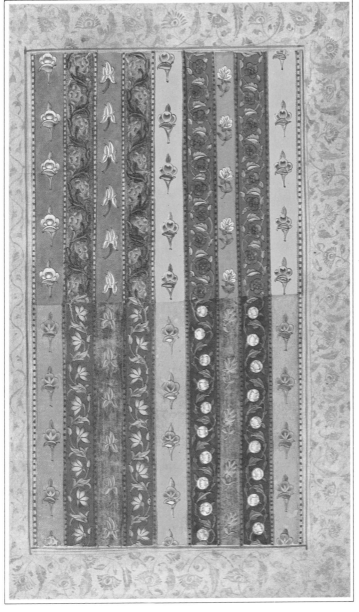

16

17

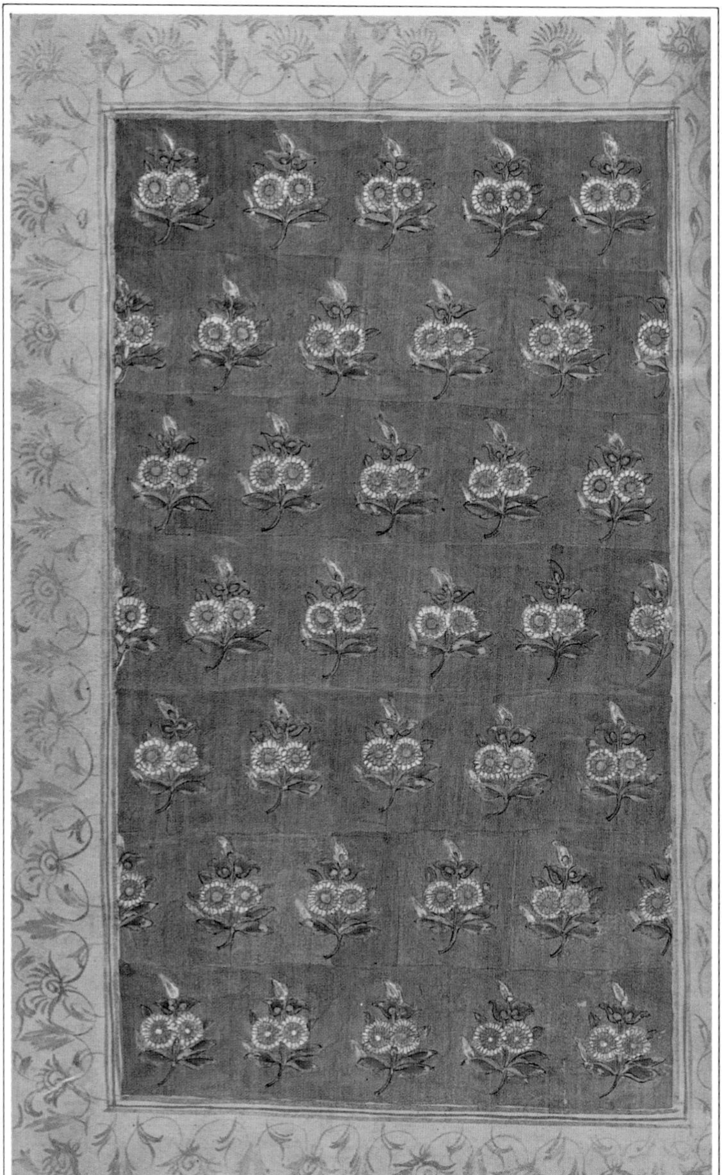

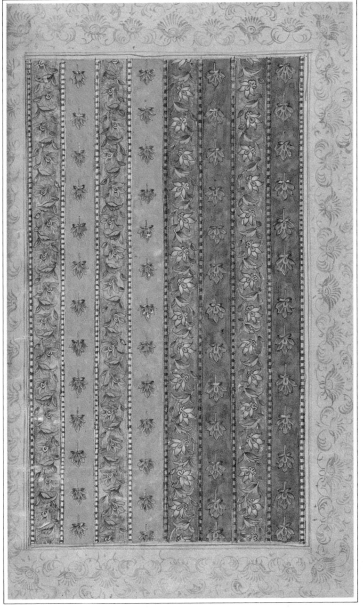

19

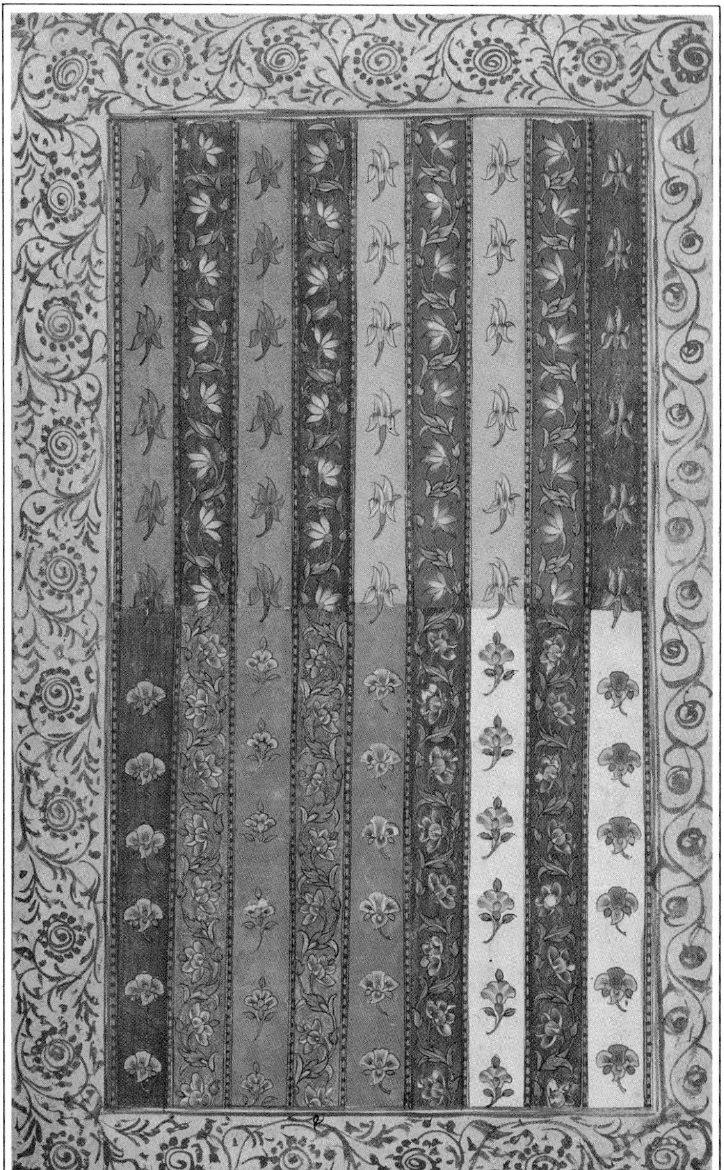

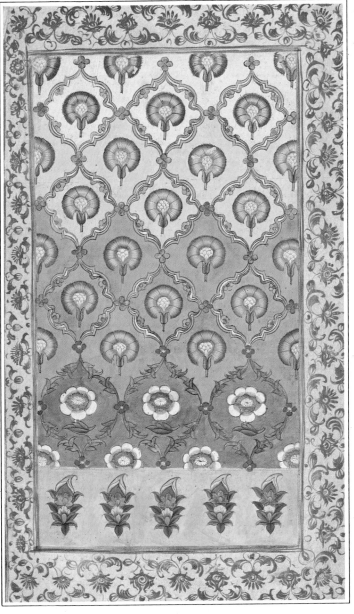

21

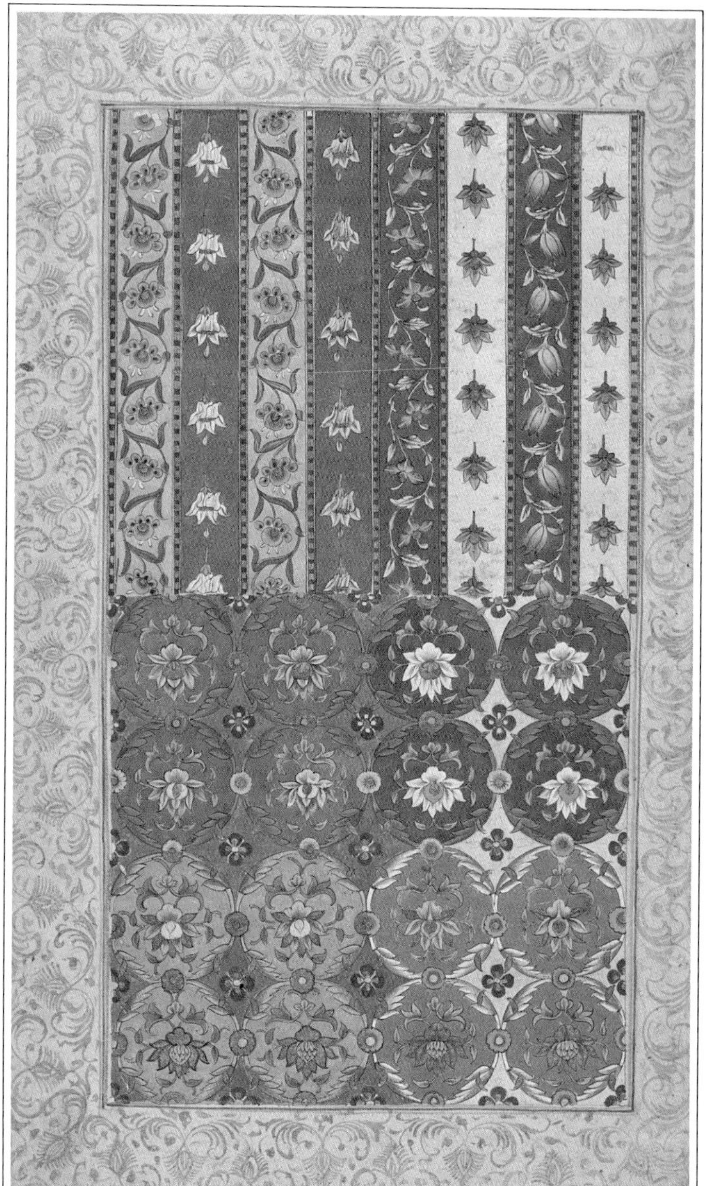

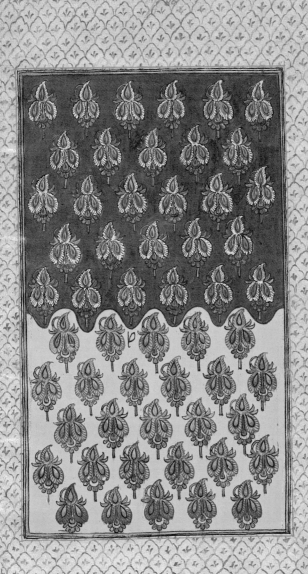

25

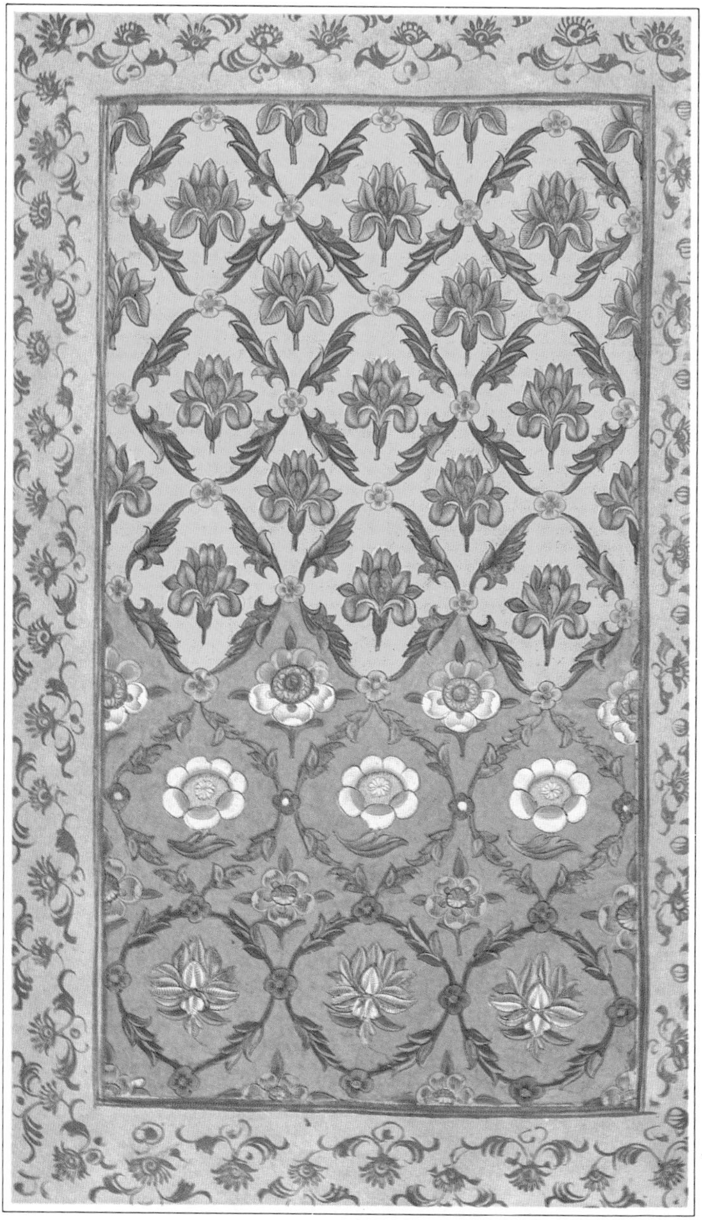

27

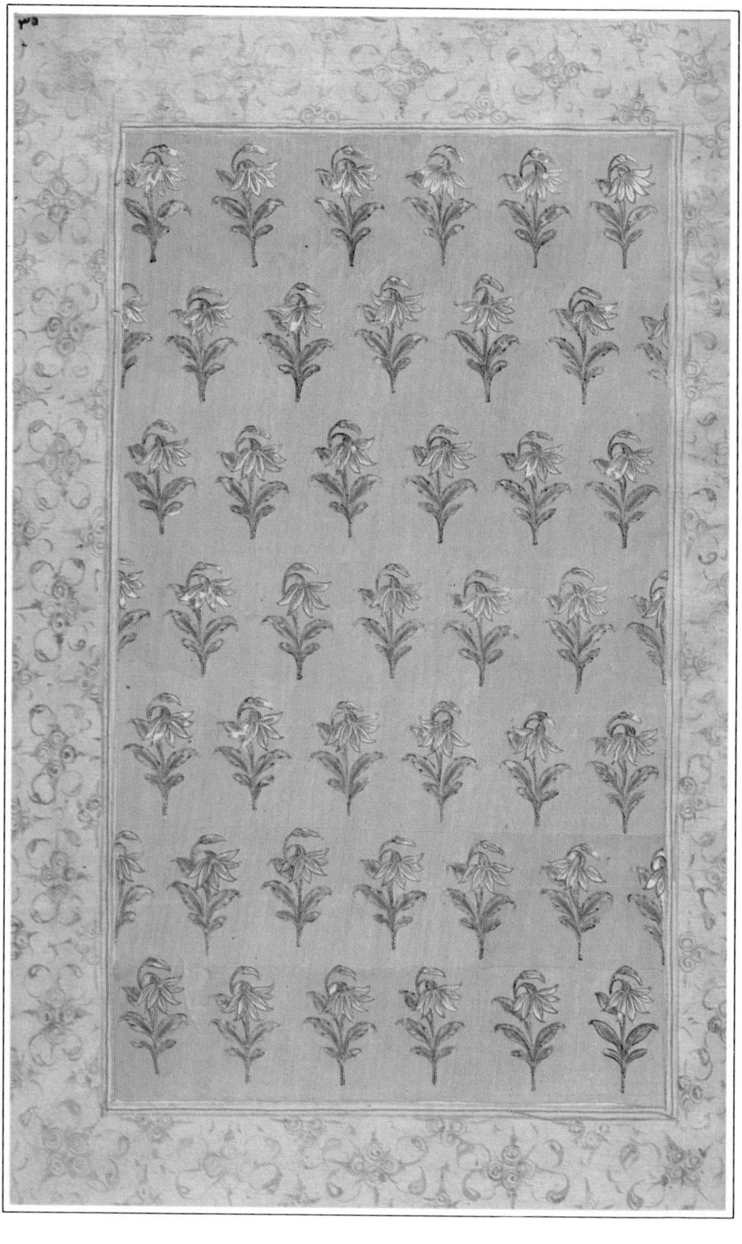

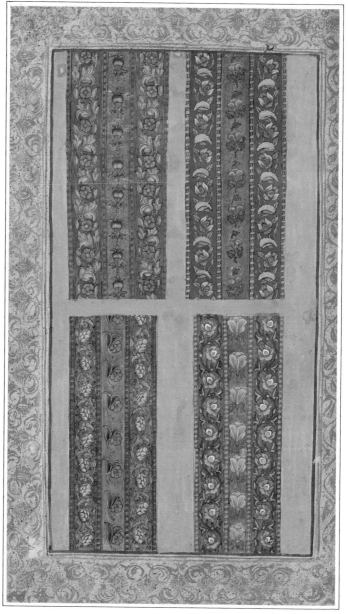

31

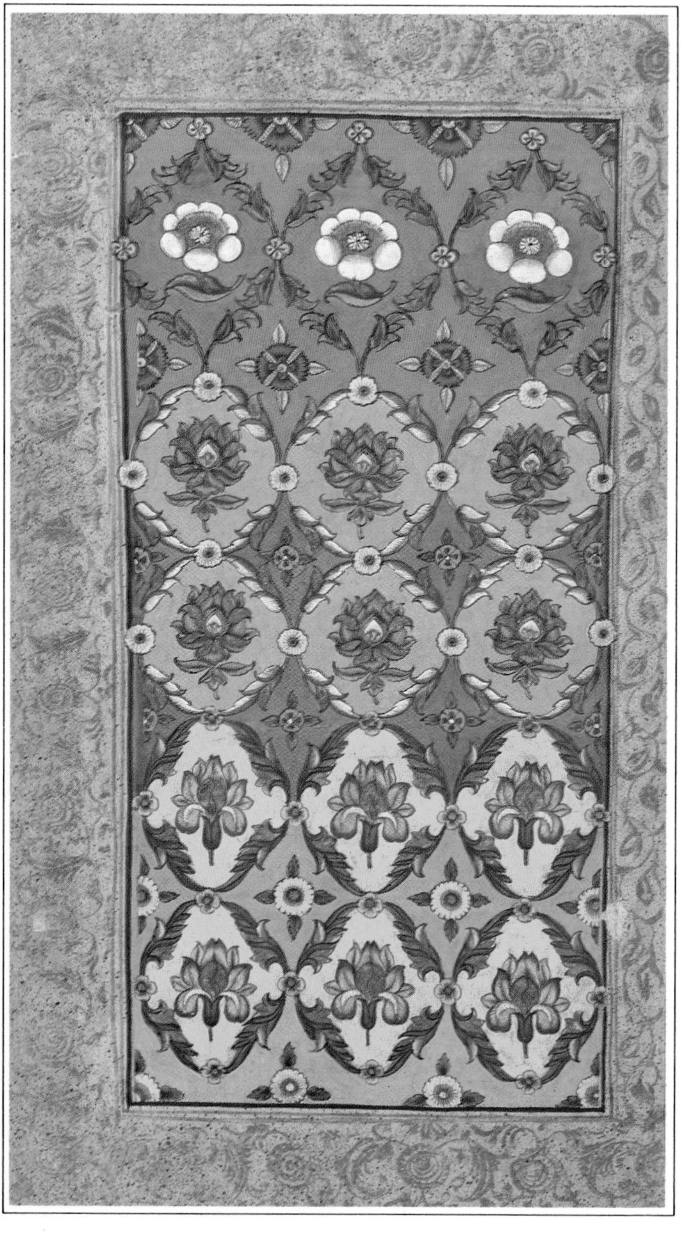